INTRO
HOLISTIC HEALTH AND RECOVERY

✳✳✳

Taking Self – Care to A Whole New Level

Author: Kathleen V Russell

Editor: Martha E Lang

ISBN: 979-8-9886841-1-4

Publisher: Holistic Health Integration Wake Forest NC

Author: Kathleen V. Russell, Wake Forest, NC

Editor: Martha E. Lang, Winston Salem, NC

Illustration Series Guidance: Michelle C. Spuck, Pawcatuck, Ct

Book Cover Design: Christina Figueroa Chicago, IL

NOTE:

This material cannot be used outside the book's copyrights without the consent of the author's written permission.

Welcome Home
Series One

Summary

- Author Sharing Her Experience Strength and Hope "Discovery in Recovery" page 8

- Identifying your shadows to find your inner light Page 9

- Connecting our relationship to Food as our integration to healing the body Page 16

- Mental Health that goes unnoticed in our Youth Page 31

- Being In the Body to meet the Spirit Finding our way home Page 47

- About the Author Page 85

Dedication

This book is dedicated to -

Generations of Grace and Collective Creative Intelligence that helped this process-

My Incredible Son, Paul J. Crossan, his wife, Kristi Lynne, and my darling Granddaughter, Angelina J. Crossan.

My beautiful daughter from another, Heather Lynn, Rich, Richie, Ryan, and Rylee Duffelmeyer

Blessings for health and healing! I wish you all "Brave Trusting Hearts!

Contents

DEDICATION — 4

CONTENTS — 6

MY JOURNEY TO GRACE — 8

SHADOWS TO LIGHT — 8
SO, WHAT WAS THE RELATIONSHIP WITH FOOD GROWING UP? — 16
WHAT IS HOLISTIC HEALTH AND RECOVERY? — 26
BEHAVIORS AND MENTAL HEALTH BEGINNING IN OUR YOUTH — 31

PREFACE: MAKING THIS BOOK YOUR OWN — 34

WITNESS YOUR HUNGER FOR CHANGE — 37

CHAPTER 1: WHAT IS HOLISTIC HEALTH AND RECOVERY TAKING SELF CARE TO A WHOLE NEW LEVEL? — 39

BODY: MINDFULNESS - BEING IN THE BODY — 41

CHAPTER 2: SPIRIT: FINDING OUR WAY HOME — 47

SOCIAL DISCOVERING PAST OR NEW FUN — 50
ECONOMICAL — 51

CHAPTER 3 — 53

WATER — 53
AIR — 56

CHAPTER 4 — 59

WHAT'S "LOVE GUT" TO DO WITH IT? — 59

How To Reduce Chemicals and Heavy Metals	62
Clean Clear Cleanse	64
Veggies Best Smoothies	65
Women's Support Signals By Removal	68
MEN'S HEALTH Internal Restoration	73
Stress: Critical Factors Highlighted	78
Hormones for Healthy Balance Care	80
CONCLUSION	**86**
ACKNOWLEDGMENTS	**89**
ABOUT AUTHOR	**96**
RESOURCES AND REFERENCES	**97**

MY JOURNEY TO GRACE

Shadows to Light

On my recovery journey that began in 1987, the support I found and continued to seek always and to this day offered me many new ideas to be willing to have an open mind to. One quote was, "Let us love you until you can learn to love yourself." I didn't know I didn't love myself; however, I always longed for availability and connection, which felt deeply elusive. Self-care and love at a new level were bright lights that opened possibilities for my inner self.

Growing up with turbulence in the home, with all the demands on expectations, was a battleground that took me far from developing anything other than how to survive. Due to the beast of Alcohol consumed by my father, the development of my young brain was blocked by continued levels of dysfunction. The precious moments of innocence were squandered by fear and intense distractions and were built into my muscles and nervous system, hard-wired!

Everything fell away as if it didn't happen. But the disturbing energy hovered around like thick tension in the air, always about to blow. As I grew older, so did my expectations to catch up with life and do what I was supposed to do. Sounds simple. Not from the environment I came from. With over-the-top insanity, fear of what's coming, and no physical escape, recovering focus and natural Inspiration were impossible. With all my best efforts, I continued to fail and felt even more lost and confused.

To survive, we conform to our environments, and the instincts that mother nature freely gifts us are hidden in the shadows. The spirit starts to fade more and more as we continue to develop our rebounds of survival. <u>Neglect</u> is widespread in dysfunctional homes or just not having the intentional time needed from our family and the adults who raise us. As we mature and develop our coping skills, we automatically sense a need to control and manipulate to save ourselves. This is partly due to the root of our misdirected wills, and our <u>false self</u> takes the driver's seat. Behaviors and habits are formed from reactions to

unhealthy environments with no one to help guide us as we get deeper into these patterns.

Our true <u>*authentic*</u> self, love, and creation are stunted and stay increasingly in hiding. Left buried deep inside the soul, we continue to try and ease our pain. The variety of influences in the world takes us on many rides to try and fit in, to be enough to be someone we are not. With additional concerns of unresolved wounds, we have created, often unknowingly, thick, deeply rooted protective walls. This has been our strength as we needed them at the times necessary. We tend not to let them down as they become a lifelong habit. We don't need to keep them up, and once we learn, we can release them as we see what is no longer needed. Some we hold on to as they are not ready to be released. It's a process of letting go, as in the one shadow at a time release once we begin a new understanding. No one will take away our right to choose whatever this means to us individually, no matter the cost. Our self-reliance and defiance are super active as it is born in dysfunctional environments. We can live there from others and create them as we make our own choices. Stopping and evaluating our decisions and how they affect us and others around me indicates how things are going. We all can get off this track if we see a pattern from a belief system that keeps us unhappy and in more pain.

So, as the world turns, we continue to make choices that recreate our troubles, as the past haunts our spirits and dictates where we go. The people who have been there and are now on the other side and healing one day at a time can help guide us if we can become even more willing and curious to see what we can find on the other side. By trying out what others have been fortunate enough to recover from.

My survival thinking and behaviors were continually unfolding, and adapting was a struggle. Whether I checked out mentally or was running away physically. I was always threatening to run away and finally did at age 15 for two weeks. I learned that we had to run for safety early in life, at age 6. My dad was always trying to keep us from leaving the house; if he drank heavily, the insanity was just too much. My mother would tell me to quietly get my catholic uniform and book bag and meet her at the car. I was frantic that we would get caught.

The brain and body were constantly firing at higher levels. With the inability to be present in adapting to school, I was left back in first and third grade; It had nothing to do with my intelligence; from testing scores and teacher's evaluations, I didn't apply myself. The lack of belief in myself was planted in the inability to focus on the classroom and fueled by fear.

I was driven by much distraction, self-image, and low self-worth, which created the darkest shadow I was alone, unable to escape.

My spirit had the wonder of healthy distractions in music, singing, dancing, art, health, sewing, and physical activities like kickball, tennis, basketball, softball, and swimming. I was super athletic and thrived on proving myself in competition with everything. I loved gymnastics in gym class and joined the basketball team during my last year in Catholic School.

Today, there is much support as professionals identify struggling students. <u>Learning Disabilities</u> (LD) and <u>Attention Deficit Disorder</u> (ADD) are the more common terms today. Society tells us to learn right from wrong. Follow the <u>Golden Rules</u>. Most people seemed to know how to adapt to life's disciplines, which was just expected in the world I grew up in. I realized that I was the <u>Lost Child</u>.

Some of the memories of my traumatic home life, living in a trauma-based environment, left me feeling constant disappointments, as my authentic self was trying to be heard but unable to break free. I just wanted someone to stop and listen to me, so I could be given the guidance I longed for. It affected every part of my relationship to building effectiveness in the classroom and trickled into all other choices that would follow. I shut down, looked out the window, and daydreamed. I drew and wrote letters.

I have a significant memory to share. Sister Josita, my 3rd-grade teacher, felt safe to me, as I was always on guard from the inside; it was part of the shadow in distraction. Her kindness, sweet energy, soft presence, and availability to see me were beautiful. Looking into my eyes with such compassion is still a memory I hold dearly. Although it may have only been a few minutes, it has lasted a lifetime.

The clear message from my own experience is profound. Along with a third grader's natural and early brain development, this teacher's qualities and ability gave me a short reprieve from my struggles. It is as if a miracle happened, as her gift to see and hear me made a huge difference. She was grounded and stood solid yet soft, and perhaps I knew I had better get it together. With no ability to concentrate and get

to this point in school, it was as if her presence and availability offered me space to find what was more profound, and I was on the honor roll that year. It is essential to share this experience as the need was strong for someone to believe in me and offer what I needed to find my way. After that year, I returned to the old ways and skated through my time in school.

Within me, I felt spiritual stagnation in sadness and buried anger, so instead, I felt better heading down the wrong roads because it was more fun, felt harmless, and felt alive and detached from the sadness I wanted to escape from. As I grew older, the troubles came in larger doses. Somehow guilt became standard, and I continued to lose my direction. That voice of good consciousness got softer, and I continued to find pleasure in getting away with whatever I could.

With my self-worth diving into the trenches, I found relief in helping others. <u>People pleasing</u> gave me the value I needed to attempt to fill in for the lack of self-love and self-care. Hiding in helping others was also a way to stay out of conflicts at all costs. I didn't speak my mind as I became afraid to somehow. Instead, I just went along with things to keep the peace. Who knew that a natural desire to help from a place within me that taught me more about experiencing warmth and kindness could become more of a distraction and survival? It seemed to become the only way I felt a sense of importance and value!

I became <u>hypervigilant</u> around my parents as the troubles continued with no hope for change. Thinking I could try and rescue my mother was always an energy I carried. I wanted her to be left alone, to have peace, and protect her from the insanity of verbal abuse. In the heart language, I felt this deeply. As my father's disease worsened, my mother was exhausted. She got support from a great medical team and attended Church more often. She was and is my hero; rebuilding her life to save ours is commendable to her beautiful soul, a true warrior.

For decades before and to our current times, the unthinkable is hard to grasp. If it threatens our security or lifestyles, the brain's denial, looking the other way, is, unfortunately, more common than we may understand if it is not our experience. Many people are lost behind closed doors, and the abuse and domestic violence victims are alarming. We cannot manage, control, or give enough to an individual with mental illness who is self-medicating and harming themselves and others!

My path on the run continued all my life, and the adrenaline running high became a natural state I lived in. I rarely could sit still. Self-Care and welcoming healing didn't happen overnight. I lived in a constant state of , and My nervous system was on overdrive. I knew I could count on my self-reliance and running; they were my strengths and kept me alive. But they also became my shadows that blocked out the incredible spirit energy on the other side of life. Trying to let someone in to help me was difficult for me. I pushed everyone away that tried to talk sense to me. It shut me down more as I didn't trust others. Instead, unfortunately, I especially shut out any authority figures that could have guided me as my lack of belief in genuine support was null and void. I was unaware that this was stunted in my childhood; however, it is a 20/20 vision now. What started as a trickle grew into a river of denial, and I was going under.

So, what was the relationship with food growing up?

Growing up, my relationship with food was relatively healthy, and like most kids, I loved candy, cookies, cake, ice cream, and soda. The best was our pastries and fresh donuts on Sundays after Church. My mother made great meals for breakfast, lunch, and dinner. Irish Catholic meat and potatoes, the occasional Italian dish she always made her sauces for, were also divine. She always made the greens and corn on the cob in the summer with tons of butter and salt. She encouraged the best of fresh seasonal fruits all year around. The best times with her nurturing were traveling in our station wagon as a family and trips to the beach. She brewed iced tea, slices of fresh lemon, fruits, sandwiches, and coolers filled with various options.

Nurturing through food is a great connection, learning new cultures around the dinner table or any mealtime. Food has a sensual element, from the presentation and aroma to the exquisite tastes to savor is incredible. Mealtimes and breaking bread are family traditions that go back to the earliest times in history and create our gatherings of love and connection. Many families have not had this experience as home life has been on many highs, lows, and inconsistencies, and perhaps this has not been the case with broken home life and other cultures. We may have been misdirected and have yet to learn how vital our nutrients are, how food matters in the way we eat, and how we need to benefit from all that food has to offer us mentally, physically, and spiritually.

Most of us have times when we turn to food for comfort. If we are emotionally affected by an event or a painful memory, we could turn to food to assist us through the more emotional upheavals to get through them. The awareness of this can become a problem if we are experiencing health issues and concerns due to the quantity or quality of foods we take in.

We eat to survive, fill up, escape, and sensualize experiences. Another part of building our relationship with food is how to nurture the simplicity of releasing much of the bondage to it. When we look at food for healing and taking self-care to another level, we add the nutrients we miss at the cellular level where it matters most. Some can be at the levels of nurturing or control, or both. Most of us need to be aware of the level of consciousness that some of these behaviors relate to unresolved, unsettled parts of our experiences.

With the current statists of obesity in our country, there is much to learn in finding healing modalities for fewer struggles and better health and well-being. Mental health and finding attention to self-care for everyone is on their journey. We have free will and the right to do as we wish. That is the problem for many of us as we become self-destructive and feed our illnesses; anger often blocks our feelings, perhaps sadness about not getting what we thought we needed. Becoming connected a bit more as we go and acknowledging these feelings is the freedom to release them. Getting them out is the key and helps many of us more than we may realize.

"The key to releasing old habits and stagnant ways of thinking is, to begin with, even a mustard seed of willingness to stay the course with others who understand."

Bedford Presbyterian Church Bedford Village, NY
All The Stars Lined Up

All the stars lined up for me to find my way to recovery in a 12-step community in Bedford Village in that beautiful Church above. They were inspiring and committed people who gave guidance from their own experience, strength, and hope. We built on the connection, love, and support I had longed for my whole life. As I mentioned in the acknowledgments at the back of this book, in 1987, my co-manager position at work offered me a new friend Robert T may he rest in peace! He and his niece Lynn walked me into my life of recovery.

On my second night, I was escorted to the Bedford Village Presbyterian Church basement, where I began to have constant spiritual awakenings. Upstairs, on the stage performance side of the Church, there was a 3- Speaker Meeting, and a woman shared her story at the podium. The silence and calmness I felt was incredible. Her message of hope through her articulate expression of love, kindness, integrity, and humor mesmerized me. I had an awakening that has never left my soul ever since. Shelly, as she referred to herself at the time, was a beautiful gift to new enlightenment that I cherish. Her influence made me aware that I was where I was meant to be. That was nearly 36 years ago, and we traveled our spiritual path daily and often spoke through the years and are thankful to stay in touch.

"NOTHING CHANGED until I healed these parts of my life through my peers who walked the walk on both sides."

The pain from this lifetime experience drove me to heal from within. Now my attraction to life is the continued unfolding of spiritual living, filled with new light and love, especially joy that continues as long as I stay awake.

Learning to do the opposite of automatic was terrific. This new skill set for healing opened the doors, windows, and many pathways that *would not have materialized* without first sharing my burdens a little at a time as I built trust and developed relationships with real caring people who stopped to listen and not dictate. So incredibly refreshing to find my way through their examples. I began to learn how to take some guidance as trust was built slowly but steadily.

When I heard I was not the wrong person, for all the lost and crazy path's I traveled, it made absolutely no sense to me. After all, I am responsible; indeed, I was an adult, but the teenager never grew up. Unresolved buried feelings felt like a loose wire firing in the air with zero grounding ability. I was sick from the environment that taught me how to survive in continuous distractions.

Turned The Corner

Faith and hope began to change my direction with people, places, and things that offered me space to believe in the calling deep within. New grounding techniques taught me that I didn't need to run anymore and that stuffing my feelings was unhealthy. Seeing a specialist in this field was another new beginning of learning this further self-care action. Learning to stop increasing my physical and mental anxiety was the same as handing me gold nuggets. I turned the corner as I gradually learned to retrain my nerves with guidance and people who understood my needs.

I spent seven years with Kathryn, a <u>Generalized Anxiety Disorder (GAD).</u> Specialist. She provided safety and was present with compassion, kindness, and understanding like no one I had ever met. She could turn on the light when I felt darkness come over me sometimes in sessions. As it turned out, by trusting her expertise, I could let go and not overmanage our time together. That was how she helped me. I listened and allowed her to offer me space and nurture me with the truth I needed to hear. My fears were mainly from the past, and I had no connection to that when I first started working with her. I have no words that can express how blessed I feel in hindsight for an excellent therapist that allowed me to the next phase of developing life skills by talking out my unsettled emotions.

I slowly began to unravel the misdirected parts of me that turned to people pleasing and wanting to help others since I thought that gave me value, so I had many years of thinking I was helping. It took much redirecting my mind to get that it is not my responsibility to fix anyone or change anyone to meet what I thought I wanted or what they needed. From my childhood in helplessness with my father and mother, I learned this in my survival. I had no coping skills other than these.

We are learning that what felt like helping hurts and can harm the natural process of someone else to find their way. Many motives are from a good place, but codependently we often cross the lines and are the last to know.

We fall with them and often don't understand why we can't help and nearly die to try and save people we love. We try to manage the unmanageable and darken our days with less self-love and self-care. So many become lost in this cycle and can't bear how dysfunctional their lives have become, beginning to think that's all they deserve. If we grow up in early childhood with all the turbulence and uncertainty, these patterns in our adult relationships are common. We can only be supportive to guide others to resources and go as far as connecting to someone willing to help by sharing that they had this walk too. Connections to people, places, and things will assist us all in healing for all members involved, including our spirits that become darkened.

Once, I was offered my self-value just by being alive, wanting to be a better person, and not feeling so lost anymore. With all the people I met with guidance and support, I could untangle the confusion, and many mountains moved as the mustard seeds began to grow. I also remembered that my mother had gone for help as she was my hero, living through all her hard times. So, although I was afraid, I was reassured I could go at my own pace, and safety was the feeling I knew I needed.

Nothing can change our past, and we may not realize how much of our lives can still block us in our present time. When we let go of some of our defensiveness, as in a slow release of air, we take in what we need a little at a time and save or discard the rest. We can put down the dukes, unclench the fist, and create positive flows of new and invigorating energy.

"Slow and Steady." Pretty amazing to shift into an open mind.

Fear is a natural feeling and tells us something is wrong. We need to pay attention to ourselves and our loved ones, who seem isolated for too long, or a change in behaviors toward ourselves and others. We are all different, and our sensitivities are unique to our experiences. We process what we need as we go and ultimately move into a level of forgiveness for healing. It happens at a deeper level than the mind trying to figure it out. Remaining curious about what could be and hope demonstrated by others around me, I took the first step. I stumbled many times but got up, wiped myself off, and continued to get love and kindness from these fantastic people.

Healing can start at any time and on any day we choose. It makes all the difference when we find self-acceptance and a sense of ease and comfort with a new process. The door to our soul is waiting for the light, and seeing our new thinking to permit ourselves to be in self-care will show us what we need.

Find your tribe, and you will never walk alone again. With passion being born, we will work harder than we did when in high gear to survive. We may grow tired from a natural growth state and experience life as it is meant to be. It feels excellent hitting the pillow at night and saying thank you for another day. I'm finally safe, and I love life and myself! Look to the light for more Grace to continue, as the gift of life is cherished each day.

What is Holistic Health and Recovery?

Holistic Health and Recovery is a substantial life-changing experience. Learning what causes adverse reactions, what we are sensitive to, and what we have been lacking in a healing journey is well worth the ride. Whatever our physical, emotional, and spiritual callings, we can begin the path to internal restoration. We logically understand that our choices determine the quality of our lives. An easier grasp of logic but without support, Inspiration, and action in maintaining our self- subscribed motivations, most of us will fall back into the old defaults, our old ways of doing things.

Part of the population is not OK there either. I learned not to assume anything and to ask questions instead. We learn so much from one another when we can listen and allow ourselves to receive and communicate our feelings and emotions in a safe place.

Finding the root cause for each person is a process; as in any recovery, our relationship to self-care and connection to new information takes time, but it works if we work it. All these new ideas will support the attention to notice when we are "Hungry, Angry, Lonely, Tired." {HALT} Each day is different as stress and lifestyles change on a dime. We can be better prepared to handle self-care with this practice daily.

For example, after many years of coaching others, I learned that many of us disconnect from the harmful effects of adrenaline related to higher activity in stress mode and how sugar, and caffeine, to name a few, have on mental, physical, and spiritual health.

We are creatures of habit, so catching ourselves is one of the most effective mindfulness practices that shift us *toward feeling our desired results.* As anxiety has a common thread with all addictions, it can be that many are unaware of how interwoven it becomes. It may have fallen into a space that is living by its demands. I also learned that my *nervous system* was always on overdrive, and It didn't take much for my body, muscle, and brain memory to kick in either. Since it was my norm, I was in self-harming mode and self-destruction for all those years. I wish I could have been taught this earlier in life. It is truly effective when we pay attention and share it with our loved ones to support one another.

I saw a psychiatrist my therapist had on the medical team in her office in my 2nd year of Intensive Psychotherapy. I was not happy with the idea of medication. I knew I wanted help, so I became willing to follow suggestions.

I surrendered and trusted that it was a good possibility that I could feel relief from the intense anxiety that was still running the show. After the first six weeks of medication and treatment, I was amazed at how much better I was doing.

I prioritized my mental health while my physical health was up and down. My deprived thoughts about not eating the good stuff due to adrenaline reactions were turned off more now that I was taking medication to calm me down. Why not allow me some treats for now? Why not *enjoy something* while therapy feels so hard? It can help on more challenging days. Allowing special healthy treats, perhaps ones that remind us of a loved one, can be an act of connection and nurturing.

Some foods may need to be avoided if they become binge foods that cause overindulgence. When I tasted a cookie or a piece of chocolate cake, it was terrific, like fireworks! As I mentioned above, I was sensitive most of my adult life to simple sugars, with noticeably increased anxiety physically and mentally. My daily food snacks slowly crept in while I was on medication, so I began eating them. It is also important to note that our body needs the right fats; pure, uncontaminated is extremely important. This lesson was in a tune of up to 40 lbs. The consequences of tuning out were the side effects that many of us have with lack of self-care, feeling bad, no energy, lack of motivation, and depression.

I woke up one day and decided that sleeping while my health was declining was no longer an option. Learning to have a new respect for my relationship with food was the first three steps, 1) Powerless, 2) Harmful and insane 3) Letting Go. I had learned firsthand how using food for comfort could shift into a physical dependency and cravings for simple carbs. I read it in books, studied it for years, and taught my clients. It is humbling to experience this powerlessness while I was in school learning the holistic health and healing l lifestyle, and today, I am grateful I did. I understand how subtle and easy it can be to go back to sleep.

When people are in the early stages of recovery, cravings can scream at them mentally and physically. Naturally, we can choose to support the withdrawal and need to be treated by medical care during extreme cases. When we shift into self-care, it is critical to understand how much negativity goes with simple sugars and the depletion of all moving parts of our nature. The crucial point is that switching our addictions is way too easy to fall into, and we can heed warnings from the right teachers and better substitutes for healthy guidance.

Recovery from mental, physical, and spiritual toxins can become a daily practice for healing each moment in the "right now." We learn to modify and simplify what best meets us *where we are today.* With education, we know as we go, and change happens. New and exciting ideas open many doors. We have "One Day at a Time," which is all we focus on. Even Better as Echart Tolle shares his gifts with the world in his book: "The Power of Now."

There are many ways to increase the quality of our health and build on our recovery roots. Healing happens with the correct treatment. Many have a history of trauma. Even one event can block our paths, usually not for another to determine. For me, I learned that I had a lot of stuffed emotions and feelings. I was in my head all the time and had no idea that buried feelings were blocking my life as an adult. Many say they have been numb and wanted to be. I didn't have this awareness; I learned to find a reason that made sense and then dismissed the rest. I said I don't care a lot, and it fell on the fibers of spiritual bankruptcy.

Many of us understand this, and adding <u>Substance Use Disorders</u>(SUD) to the family mix gets more complicated. Love is there, but so much is lost in the chaos. It felt like my fault because I didn't follow the rules. You made the bed, now lie in it, was a joint statement in those days, further increasing isolation and lack of understanding pushed me further away. With addiction leading, life stays in these cycles and is progressive. We often don't understand why and underneath it all, we are confused about so much but don't know how to change it. It seems obvious to others in our life that we need help, but instead of listening to anyone, we turn them away.

The medical field now recognizes addiction as <u>mental health disease.</u> Although anyone with addiction is buried deep under the genuine and authentic self, we don't believe we are at fault for these experiences that shaped our pain and hurt and caused much of our need to build survival skills to cope. How amazing we can rise in such freedoms to light when we learn to be open, willing, and honest on a new pathway. We walk free together as it offers the authentic self to be born, as in a rebirth to life we didn't know how to find. We can have several renewals as new awakenings to a pure natural beginning.

Behaviors and Mental Health beginning in our Youth

Could we be missing something in our young ones? Were these concerns missed when we were younger and still unknown today? A fundamental factor is that many of our brains lack the chemicals needed for emotional stability. Are we born with less, or has our trouble come from environmental exposure, or have both become an issue over time? What do we know about these issues, especially if no one has experience with them? When this is missed, as it often can be, the individual is judged harshly and frequently punished. When the behavior is related to <u>Trauma and PTSD,</u> a child cannot conform or focus at these moments, hours, or days when it is activated. Adults are in the same challenges with unresolved deeper hurts that still interfere without specific support to help. With these signals we see in our loved ones, we can find much healing at the deeper levels, and beginning as early as possible, we can be free to explore and grow as we deserve.

A significant and sometimes life-saving for some of the younger generation is the fact that there is a need for healing and getting to know a person we work with. Over time we find a solution and the correct answers for our experience. Going to a doctor for a pill for any reason, in my humble and experienced past, is not a safe path. Many children and parents are unaware that brain chemistry will be altered, and many deaths are related to medications-altering mental stability. Please know the risks and have a good team in all areas to support you and your loved ones.

All the valuable lessons we have been through have become our way of

helping others, and our compassion for one another grows as we pass it on. Honestly, there is no more fabulous gift than to be an instrument in this way. After some healing that happens as we look within and get support, *discernment becomes the gift that follows.* New freedoms unfold and will offer us so much. This <u>Amazing Grace</u> video expresses this beautifully.

Light Within... May you find yours Now

Preface: Making this Book Your Own

I am very grateful to have the opportunity to write this book. I have been working on it through the isolation of Covid 19 for over three years. It helped me heal unexpectedly and stay as close to sane as possible. I am grateful and passionate about sharing the many opportunities to live a holistic lifestyle with others. Instead of thinking about being selfish in a negative perspective or feeling guilty when we put ourselves first, we can learn how rich life can become, learning how to nurture all our functionality. We will begin to experience how much self-care helps us to, in turn, be more available to our loved ones. Putting the acid to the test and finding new freedom to authentic care for all concerned is remarkable, and I hope to assist you on your way.

The old-fashioned pen-to-paper helps free up new space to reflect on. Journaling can offer much contemplation, and writing is beneficial to bringing awareness to healing and new freedoms. Have fun with it; find whatever makes you feel connected, safe, loved, and valued. What do you need to recognize in yourself that perhaps you have forgotten? Paste, draw, or paint as you create new awakenings. Learning to be curious will help lighten it up and give you further questions. Create your space to offer comfort and peace for a quiet self-care time.

The guidance in this book will teach you how the healing journey within helps restore and rebuilds the capacity you can personally push through. Much of our success happens as our spirits shine and we "try on" new ideas that keep us feeling pretty good, inside and out. A trial run will give you personal power from experience firsthand. You will hold onto what fits and wade through the rest as the process unfolds. Turning on and tuning into the relationship between emotions and physical reactions is the stage for our systems' mental, emotional, and physical digestion. Our spirits become more enlightened to awakenings as we explore what speaks to us.

Spending time alone is part of making space for our reflections and processing what we are going through at different seasons as we connect with our new levels of healing and self-care, self-love, and valuing our lives. We find much enlightenment as we work together in reflections on who our human guides were as we grew up and now. Even keeping our world small, if that is more comfortable, is only the shadow if we isolate ourselves for protection instead of quiet needs for a good balance. When we can begin to seek our truth and stay honest with ourselves, if we move through certain blocks that often feel like this is as good as it gets, there are new lights within that we still need to meet.

Suggestions will start to stimulate new thinking. As you learn what speaks to you, take notes for your memory later. It is more common for our brains to dismiss ideas before we try something new. As you catch this new wave of thinking, remember to ride it out. Try recent actions and stay curious, tapping into all senses and sensitivities.

If you have the book in hand, make notes to yourself in the columns to find later. Highlight with colors of importance to meet you where you are today. What speaks to you TODAY? If you are learning from the internet, I encourage you to buy the book to have it ready. Having the book for guidance and references have the impact needed for inspirational reminders. You will learn what fits you best as you combine it now and later. I encourage you to read with new and fresh eyes and put aside the critical brain. Be open and pure of heart and spirit.

Science tells us that we live 90% from our unconscious mind, and much of what we do is automatic. We each live from experiences that have influenced us on our journey. Being mindful is the path to positive new messages we can choose.

The gift of continued Grace, light love, and any other feelings that come and become a part of understanding the Ebb and Flow of life, as all are important to find our authentic light and a more profound joy that may have only been in the thought life or desire to find out there—guidance daily to keep growing and finding new ideas. Has been blessed for three decades in action, and I enjoy the results of my Higher Calling. Many generations in recovery who raised me and have been passed down through Grace we all share on his journey. We find loyalty in our life- saving spirits as we heal daily with deep appreciation and gratitude.

Witness Your Hunger for Change

I have been incredibly bright in my spirit as I have witnessed, coached, and sponsored many amazing, courageous people. The chance to have turned around the quality of their lives and to see their hunger for change is outstanding. Many of us have been blown away by our new experience. By taking more initiative, we help ourselves and seek support to stay the course. Think of what *you can do rather than what you can't.* We begin to connect the dots as the relationship with the mind, body, and spirit and will offer the natural integration process.

As we practice living more in the moment, the positive energy and good feelings that follow from our decision to feel better is the change we want to make. Your new efforts to make small changes matter and you will notice that your actions will help give you more Inspiration. All things are possible when we believe and ask for what we need. This will be a pleasant surprise if you have never been in a setting for professional coaching to walk you through what you need support with.

The guidance, support, and intuition offered with live coaching are the Grace I have become dedicated and loyal to from all the fantastic opportunities I said Yes to and gave everything I had. Once the light stayed on, a new flow of energy kept me inspired and in acceptance of the darker moods and more challenging days. It is part of life, and I now know that I was a victim in my past but a volunteer in my adult life

since my shadows were blamed on my history and others even in life before I knew better.

Whatever you are dealing with has become too much to tackle on your own; now, healing with time and safe space will be provided for you. It takes the commitment to open our minds to new ideas and learn; we are OK with asking for nurturing, understanding, and love where and when we need it. Applying some of these steps to *discovering* a good fit for you to heal all parts is your fresh start and a new beginning.

Chapter 1: What Is Holistic Health and Recovery Taking Self Care to A Whole New Level?

Holistic Health is an authentic relationship to self, an integration *of* all our functioning systems when tapping into the Mind, Emotions, Body, Spirit, Social, and Economical, which is the book's nature. We require a better balance internally, which gives a maximum state of homeostasis and is needed at multi-levels.

In this first series details the harmful effects of low levels of natural cleansing support, some internal build-ups are unwanted synthetic and unnatural chemicals that denaturize our cells from everyday things we do or don't do. We walk mindlessly and fall into line with three great mysteries of life, a fish can't see the water, birds can't see the air, and humans can't see themselves.

The great news is that we will alter and shift the internal environment. We Learn to tap into the connection with oneself and find that self-care is not just a rare event but a daily practice. We will gradually add to and increase the

quality of our lives. A message about manifesting our lives by

the power of suggestions, as in, **The Law of Attraction,** provides a letter for displaying our passions.

As I continue to learn and apply to my daily walk, I focus on deeper needs for my truth and its manifestation of them; even if I don't feel it at the moment, I continue to practice this anyway. I may think I will get somewhere in the thought life, but without action, those thoughts are left dangling in the air somewhere soon to be forgotten. Common sense says we lack experience, so it may be a reason we come up with true or not; we create the dead end for ourselves.

Many of us have high demands with our responsibilities to work and family. We may have very long hours, whether caregiving or trying to juggle work and family; it can take a toll on us. This will affect the stress levels we experience and could have many side effects that we may not be aware of.

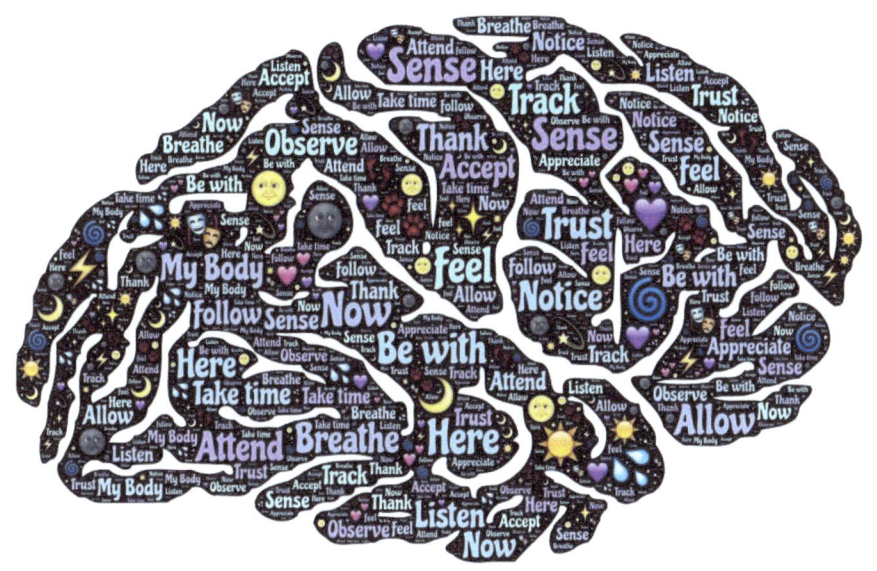

Body: Mindfulness - Being in the Body

How far away do you live from your body?

The physical body and how much we struggle with it are linked to how much attention we give to our functionality. Our body is unique to our DNA, past experiences, and daily choices. It is profound how much neglect and abuse our body puts up with. A change of thinking around the relationship to healing will open windows of opportunity to shift internally. We can offer the natural response and flow of energy and healing in many ways that are not complicated, habits to learn toward healing the positive flow of good energy in us and around us. Becoming open, more in tune, and aware of what we can experience will become a new mission in restoration.

Many choose to find healthy options to assist the body in releasing the toxins that linger around and hide in the body. The body has a natural process to remove them <u>through the organs,</u> for example, our lungs, kidneys, liver, and skin. Our <u>brain</u> also has a detoxing process while we sleep. It is a standard process for many clients to choose their unique treatments to support themselves for cleansing. Our organs, to be sure nothing, is getting in the way of rebuilding our cellular growth. We can detox as a first step to giving ourselves the best options to absorb, rebuild and feel better.

We can find what is best to meet us where you are now, taking just one step at a time. Learning to think differently takes time to happen. You may want to dive right in and be ready to be a little uncomfortable for a while is entirely up to you and guidance to meet you where you are now. It will depend on your current health conditions and your health team to decide what is best for your health and well-being.

The strength begins at the cellular level based on nutrients' density and absorption. It is about something other than thinking we are doing our best. As the levels go deeper, so does the need. I have heard many excuses or limited satisfaction to a false sense of security in all walks of life. One example is taking an over-the-counter (OTC) vitamin a day. Many think this is enough and are offered peace of mind, but it is a limited understanding of healthy options. Many over-the-counter vitamins have Binders, Fillers, Dyes, Chemicals, and contaminants, which are also in our food and supplement supply, so It all Matters!

Without understanding this, we become depleted, which shows in the side effects we just learned to live with. So many people blame anything on old age as the primary and very acceptable excuse to assist in our denial.

It is so easy to be stuck in this line of thinking, and you can easily see why we can lose our motivation. It becomes a real stagnation as the central beavers continue to work. We are accelerating our disease states and premature aging in these stagnating places. Remember that our body stores negative energy, creating shadows that block our way. Our physical body/ mind connection is linked to people developing illnesses that can become life-threatening. Think Clean Clear Cleanse for new habits to natural detoxing as a way of life. This is the best line of defense. It may not be easy, but it's always worth it!

The standard procedure of going to the doctor to fix things for us is limited to how much we do for ourselves. They can't feed us or make us take better care of ourselves. Being cautious of recurring problems is the body's way of trying to tell us something. Pointing our fingers at the

doctors is taking the responsibility away from ourselves. It is not their job to keep us healthy. They can only go as far as their education takes them. Combining medical and holistic medicine is the best way to heal all the parts we struggle with. Think about the number of people in our elder community diagnosed with Dementia, Alzheimer's, Heart Disease, or Cancer.

With <u>Diabetes</u> as an example, the main concern becomes a physical and mental <u>addiction to simple sugars and Alcohol.</u> It is the same as cocaine; our brain releases feel-good endorphins when we eat sugar. Our physical craving for more simple sugars triggers us to eat more of them, which, in turn, starts a cycle into an unhealthy balance in reaction to them.

With life being difficult at many turns, we naturally look for a release or, at times to escape. The desire to enjoy our simple pleasures is essential and needed in self-care and healing. Commonly and frequently, we turn away from people who try and help offer guidance.

It can feel more like control coming at us, and defending ourselves is much stronger at these times. Finding honesty is the last thing at that moment, as we usually don't care. It is none of anyone's business. This is so true, but be careful with the attitude of defiance in these challenging times, as it often is a block that doesn't support change. It is all about the philosophy and self-honesty that will make the difference in our health concerns and the physical healing we choose to be in our favor.

Many depend more on doctors to get the pill to fix the illness. We can quickly think it's a free pass to do what we want, a self-harming self- destructive behavioral pattern. It is no different from someone who needs oxygen due to smoking attached to a tank and still smokes, an addiction like all others. Even when you think you are improving, the body has a different reality.

Society has a way of adding emotional guilt and shame, which makes us *stay in hiding.* With the judgment of self and others, we are blocked and often stuck in these feelings. We become lost in adjusting ourselves to these lower powers and often live on in them without the intervention of support. We can carry them as a visceral feeling in the body, and often many have attached them to the trauma they have been through. No matter what it may be related to, if it stays in the dark, it stays in the body.

Learning what you can be missing or not absorbing will open a pathway to healing as you understand what you need to add to necessary foods, supplements, or medication. What little beavers are building dams in you? If you want to prevent the onset of diseases, learning some new norms will help you get results. You will need to bear some facts about the underlying troubles that begin with the lack of Nutrient Dense foods that work with our body and the elimination of the ones that don't.

Most of us would change things if we didn't feel alone or lost in some of these behaviors and habits. Becoming mindful and learning to tune in and tap into our body will teach us how to connect the body to our present moment. We don't need to stay stuck. Once we learn there are options, it becomes easier to find answers. For example, it is not customary to be uncomfortable and reach for drugs to feel better. We have lost our way, and illness is the direction if we don't take new action.

People who are not feeling well for whatever reason, emotionally, mentally, physically, or spiritually, can begin to find the light. Progress, not perfection, helps us stay hopeful and keeps us realistic. Being hard on ourselves with struggles doesn't allow for healing; it only invites more turmoil. Learning to be kind, gentle, and loving is needed, and looking for ways to remind yourself of this is essential. If you must beat yourself up, use a feather instead. All you need is a mustard seed of Inspiration; keeping the faith, you will find the rest as you go.

Chapter 2:

Spirit: Finding Our Way Home

What does the spirit of a human being mean to you? How do you spend time with your spirit? Do you have a daily practice of ways to tune in and tap into yourself? Do you have good people's support to allow your vulnerabilities to be expressed and released? Finding our authenticity is often the quiet voice we don't allow to lead or guide us. Our minds and desires often shut them down. Paying attention to them is our way of awakening to healing and joy.

When it comes to spiritual guidance, it is often confusing as it can be interwoven with the Church, and both seem to have the same meaning. Some combine Spirituality with Religion when looking up information. For many people, it can block our healing of authentic self. Spirituality can be considered many things once we look beyond what we know about this healing. Our choices are many, and we must find what feels right.

Spirit is the short word for spirituality. We often hear Mind, Body, and Spirit throughout the many ways of self-care. Learning to be still, quiet our mind and connect to our wholeness is sometimes challenging. Our spirits come to life when we find what helps us communicate better. Our voices can be heard from within as we explore what reaches our hearts. Visiting Buddhist monasteries, various sanctuaries, retreats, sitting by the water listening to the waves, and taking in the incredible aroma of the sea, are some excellent ways to tap into self and spirit. Finding this place within can be a practice we do wherever and whenever we need to.

Self-talk reinforces the truth as we know it from this place within. This approach is one of the best tools we can use and is sharpened daily as our needs change.

We can be excited about our lives and deserve the freedoms of life through our spiritual selves. Allowing a sense of ebb and flow helps to create positive energy and reduce the negativity rigidity gives. The message to self can feel like a refreshing fountain of our Youth. As we grow spiritually, we learn to shed our survival tools. We begin to see new visions and senses and experience life at a deeper level of joy and happiness.

Learning that anything that blocks us from being "Open Minded" can affect our overall health and healing is incredible. But conversely, a closed mind causes stagnation in our lives. If we are rebelling, who is being punished?

Scheduling and definitive planning, as part of a routine to step out of all the activity, allows us the space to listen for our spirit voice within, to teach us what it desires us to know. Looking for what inspires us and helps us to get out of ourselves is a pathway to finding our Authentic selves. Our spiritual human experiences come from within!

Shifting from _defiance_ is a big step toward our truth and freedom. Many people have become autopilot default; our stories become our deep convictions on how we see things. As we move into a gradual level of acceptance to reflect on some new ideas, it teaches us to listen to what the spirit self has to say. The work from spirit, a mental bypass, sets us free of some rigidity. Learning that our spirit is not all about religion is an excellent place to start. Some have eventually combined their childhood faith and found the light within the soul, but many have not.

Simple things we can do for the spirit to connect to our health and well- being is being outdoors with nature. Barefoot on the ground can increase the body's energy from the earth. Our hands in the dirt with projects, from upgrading projects to gardening, is good for the soul. So, take advantage of the beautiful days to be outside and enjoy the senses of all that nature offers.

Social Discovering Past or New Fun

Having fun is an area that many of us need help with busy lives, work schedules, and family obligations. Vacation time may be the limited social time we get. Playhouses or art museums are extraordinary to stroll through. We can use the resources of vendors and small businesses to support locally, and some of them join the Chamber of Commerce, where much is posted on their website. Libraries, Law enforcements, Fire Departments, American Legend, and VFWs, have significant events to gather, as we can show up to support our first responders in service.

Book Clubs Pottery classes Humm What would you like to try? Signing lessons or music classes Nice to think of what may inspire new spiritual lights to open your joy inside. Then, of course, line dancing can be part of the Studio's gyms or the YMCA. Cafe folk music is offered in barn houses and the like.

Reminders of the things that brought you joy and simplicity growing up can be invented. We still have a kid inside that is very much alive and well. It is one of the gifts we can tap into; even if we recall less from times in our Youth, we can kindle new ideas that offer us a bright spot in our lives today. That is where our spirits become alive and teach us more about ourselves in the here and now, regardless of biological age. Keeping a youth-like spirit can be missed if we lose this connection somewhere along the journey; however, it is always there to assist us in our healing when we try. Please keep it simple, make it fun (KISMIF) was a slogan I heard in a live 12-step meeting, and it changed my course of thinking so much about how I felt at that moment. I realized It had a lot more to do with my attitude and how I could shift my thinking and feel much lighter more often than not. When I felt the darkest in recovery, which surprisingly moved my spirit and healed many parts of my shadows, journaling can help bring new ideas you haven't thought of.

Economical

How much attention do we pay to our ecosystems? From our homes to the largest of scales, we, as a community, can inspire one another for the greater good.

Our global concerns are evident with much information from our agricultural studies. All aspects of our lives and people committed to saving our earth go to great lengths for necessary investigations. Simple cooperation has been implemented, and recycling is mandated in our current times. This could be an entire book of its own as well as each of the topics I discuss; however, in the context of holistic health, it is important to add each of the ways to our holistic health and healing that takes self-care to another level.

There is still a percentage of people who comment or add to social media things like, "Oh, everything is terrible for you" statements, and I wonder how we lived through all the things we did and survived. "Or these contaminants are everywhere." Simple things make a difference; the effort is wise for healthy living.

An incredible amount of new chemicals have been introduced since my childhood. Our faster-paced instant gratification has taken control over all aspects of our lives at all levels. The conditioning of this mindset has been a slow but steady pace of health decline. Have you stopped to realize how so much has changed, and we stay asleep as if we don't have options?

Much of this information is available as we dig to get to the truth at the higher levels. However, when it relates to our healthy options, it needs to begin with us. Learning what we are doing without questioning needs to shift, and the willingness to learn and grow in a new light is the support we all need today.

Chapter 3

Chilled Lemon Lime and Mint for 24 hours

Water

I f you were alive in the 1960s, you might remember the question, What's in your water? It was a joke in the old days as if the water made us act silly or delirious. We would always have a good laugh.

We need water to service a natural healing need and operate all our functioning operation systems. Many people have been dehydrated for years, even worse, decades. There are basic needs daily for purifying our water and in the amounts needed for mear survival.

So many of the symptoms we have are due to dehydration.

Here are some symptoms you may have without adequate intake of water:

- Lack of absorption
- Fatigue
- Depression
- Anxiety
- Headaches
- Bloating
- Muscle soreness
- Joint tenderness, pain, and inflammation
- Kidney problems
- High Blood Pressure
- The onset of illness over time

Of course, there can be complex concerns for each of us, and one thing doesn't cover all bases. However, it is essential to be clear that these concerns are real without adequate water intake and must be addressed to prevent further complications. Our kidneys alone need 2 cups of water to work for us. Drinking water overall is required for every single organ and healing. Just like the air we breathe, we can't live without it. It is astounding that so many people get by with so little intake. It is essential to learn hy as to gauge the levels needed daily. It is mentioned in a few places as reminders and simple to do. Whatever your Current Body Weight (CBW), cut that number in half, which is how many ounces you need daily.

Plastics are made with phthalates, parabens, BPA, and the top 3 other chemicals. Science has warned us that these chemicals are leaching into food and beverages, and we ingest them daily. The temperature variations are also something to be aware of. Many people buy bulk cases and store them in uncontrolled environments like garages and the back of vehicles until needed. The temperatures fluctuate, encouraging chemicals to be released more. These invisible invaders get into our bodies and brain. Scary, right?

It is incredible how much we learn as the investigations continue with specialists in our health field. In the microwavable style world, we have adapted to consume much more of what is depleting our health, and many of us need more direction to get enough on the other side of the scale to balance our healthy state.

It is essential to make an effort to find purified and quality water. Our tap water is not what it used to be, and in today's world, nothing is! There are many options on the market today. A whole house filtration system is the way to go if you can afford it. From bathing to showers to cooking to drinking, all purification is the best well-rounded and plentiful purity you can offer yourself and your family. It is an investment that you will most likely be pleasantly surprised as to how much better your hair, skin, and health shift.

Learn the best options within your budget and know you have the purest water to clean, clear, and cleanse the mind and body for thriving and the best health.

Dangerous contaminants in our water are a concept introduced previously. Still, it is important to note that the requirements by the city standards differ from the purity your body strives for. The facts are that much of the tap water has nitrates, mercury, lead, and trihalomethanes, to name the chemicals and contaminants that can still be in our drinking water and bathing is also a concern as now we know that our skin absorbs what we use topically. I started giving our fur babies the best water to prevent contaminants, as they, too, can be at risk.

AIR

From the chemicals outside to the ones we bring in, we are depleting the air quality we breathe, and the <u>oxygen levels</u> in today's world are much lower than in the old days. We can't stop the flow of new substances around us, but we can try not to use them in our daily choices to help invest in our health and support our environment. All our collective decisions can help make a significant impact on the whole. The green living options are growing daily for the alarming ozone deterioration. Let's hope we can all make better choices and understand the severity of this for the generations that follow.

It may not even be conscious for many of us to learn that some of our choices can reduce the air quality we breathe. Many people are not aware of the benefit it can bring to their health. The air we breathe indoors, where we spend most of our time, makes a huge difference, and this awareness will increase our oxygen levels. Our air quality today affects our health, and simple things can help immensely.

To help increase the oxygen levels for ourselves and our families, and the workplace, here are some things we can do:

- Ceiling and floor fans
- Varieties of humidifiers prevention of dry air (Helps our furniture breathe too)
- Air purifiers with frequent filter checks
- Environmentally and proven safe cleaners (Research doesn't trust labels alone)
- Open windows in the am or late in the day
- Venting the air when cleaning

Perhaps you are already using earth-friendly cleaners. That is great! If you still need to, it is essential to learn your best options. There are so many studies now that connect the adverse effects. We don't see them, so who knew, right? Now we know that they can stick around for days after we clean. I always thought many were natural, but I have learned otherwise. It is important to vent the air when cleaning to prevent inhaling and scaring our lungs.

Chapter 4

What's "Love Gut" to Do With it?

Everything...... <u>Our second brain is in our gut,</u> *large and in charge.* Detoxing from all synthetic chemicals is vital as they interrupt our healing and increase our anxiety and digestion issues. We come in contact with many chemicals that deplete these good gut supporters through the air, water, food, and personal products.

Our digestion system starts in the mouth and ends in elimination. Simple right? Our body detoxes all the time.

To what degree our toxins and synthetic chemicals are released is related to the health of our gut. Unfortunately, without attention to details like the digestion needs and best cleaning methods, we are missing the absorption of much-needed nutrients. We can be missing not in the pure and cleansing category daily. Many people struggle with things as simple as not drinking enough water, which causes a domino effect that moves us into health concerns. It's like the beaver that blocks the dams. When we learn how to do the simple things to keep things moving at least once or twice a day and add fermented foods to feed our guts. The way for support is a company that is third-party tested. I am happy to offer guidance and tips on where to look. I invite you to contact me at my email address for questions at [holistichealthrecovery87@gmail.com.](mailto:holistichealthrecovery87@gmail.com)

The best healing happens, and moods are better as we naturally begin to make our serotonin to assist our overall good state of well-being.

Natural "gut guys" fill their environments with the [microbiome](), friendly gut guys, and Pro and Prebiotics. They are needed for proper nutrient absorption, kick the bad guys out, and eliminate and remove them through natural detox. Keeping our guts clean allows the body to cycle in a natural detox. Note that anxiety and depression have become common responses to an unhealthy gut. This is because serotonin, the neurotransmitter related to mood, is made in the gut.

Many foods help the gut increase the level and quality of <u>these good guys naturally and effectively.</u>

It is good to take one day of the week and set aside time to reflect on simple ideas through your busier times in the week. Then look ahead to when you have more time to explore new ideas and ways to increase the quality of your Holistic Health styles.

To add foods, you can look for Keifer drinks and be forewarned if you are Alcohol and drug-free. Some have alcohol content from the fermentation process; for example, Ginger options usually are a concern for alcohol content. I made that mistake as my foggy brain and free-floating anxiety followed a thirsty summer day. Dairy and coconut are usually Alcohol-free, and their benefits are nutritious and health- friendly.

How To Reduce Chemicals and Heavy Metals

It may seem overboard to replace our homes with healthier daily options; however, we can slowly alter some of our everyday things to prevent adding more metals to our bodies. We can take this to any level that fits our lifestyles. If we are older, we can be assured that any steps we take may increase our longevity and be a positive step in preventing the concerns from years of toxic levels.

So let's look at our <u>pots and pans that are metal and chemical-based</u> and replace them with natural cast iron and glassware for the best results for daily use. We can also use parchment paper or paper inserts in muffin tins to not absorb the metals when baking. It can be more practical and straightforward enough. Replace your toxic cleaners with other cleaners that are environmentally safe to use in your environment. Choosing the more natural product for our hair and skin offers the best way to reduce the toxic overload we carry internally.

Your body is always attempting to fight for you, which alone can tire us as it tries to prevent illness from synthetic toxins that are not welcome. We are always in a state of healing and cleansing.

We are often surprised at the incredible ability our body has for healing. Yet, to the very nature of our beings, we are the ones who benefit as we pay attention, do all we can, and then look to our doctors to help in assistance as required. As we are honest with ourselves and take responsibility for our choices, we will also be honest with the doctors to help treat us better.

It is wise to re-consider all our daily activities that could increase the exposure to the metals we take in. Our skin alone is a sponge to all externals, as we have known with the use of patches for pain and other health considerations.

I have assisted many families in making simple changes to do what they need and not add toxic chemicals that seem relatively harmless because they smell pretty. For example, adding shampoos as a new idea that helps treat the hair and scalp with the nutrients they need can be absorbed. I had not given that too much in the old days, and if we wash our hair daily with these chemicals, we may consider trying some things safer. Lotions, creams, and makeups are also available in healthier options, so if that interests you, you may be surprised at what you can find.

We become aware of some of our daily activities and can quickly help reduce these levels.

Clean Clear Cleanse

Keeping the mantra of Clean Clear and Cleanse will remind you that you can make new choices to feel better and protect your stagnation internally. A great way to help remove toxins from the body is through the healthy nutrients and minerals in our plant life. Since it is seemingly the more depleted part of the American habit to have enough of the veggies on the dinner plate or a small side salad, we miss the levels that offer maximum benefits for health. Along with a Multi-Vitamin and Mineral to fill in the cracks, these can be a great way to enjoy a refreshing smoothie with rich organics. You can also add a mix of the greens that are condensed versions that I am happy to share with you as well.

Veggies Best Smoothies

Smoothies are a popular source of drinking nutrients. Remember to stay within a portion size for good balance and to prevent sugar overload. Adding some protein and a veggie or two is a great way to make it healthy and taste better than veggies alone for some people. We can add these to smoothies or drink a shot of super greens. Large generous 3-6 cups salads are a great way to get your daily greens and minerals that often can be lacking.

An incredible amount of new chemicals has been introduced since then. Our faster-paced instant gratification is taking control over all aspects of our lives, and the conditioning of this mindset has been a slow but very steady pace of a health decline.

It is astounding how much of the food chain has genetically

engineered organisms in our fruits and veggies from the sprays in farmer's fields. There are connections to cancer and so much more ill health from these chemicals that stay in the body and tear down our cellular function. Non-GMO is offered, and I will get into that further in the section I cover.

We have alarming levels of toxic metals from the water and earth. What about the food supply we eat and the medications we take when needed? Have you thought about the incredible rise in so many diseases and disorders of our time today? Alzheimer's has become an enormous concern in the 20th century. Have you ever connected the possibility that these heavy metals floating around in the brain assist in the decline and vulnerability to the health of our brain?

All these foods are healthy and supportive to the average person looking for the building blocks to staying strong. Please be reminded that all things are not suitable for all people with special conditions that you and your medical team are working on. It is essential, especially because some medications have negative and severe interactions. It is important to run things by those who know your health for up-to-date safety.

Science warns us about chemicals leaching into our food from plastic containers while cooking and with temperature variations. This often includes frozen packaging. We can use safer options like Pyrex or Cast Iron.

Then we question whether the nutrients are lost in microwave cooking. Here is what Harvard studies say. I have heard that microwave cooking denaturalizes the natural benefits of foods. Many people in the south use slow cooking options like low temp smokers for 20 hours for tender, tasty meals, and family dinners.

Women's Support Signals By Removal

So how can we know what is going on? Eliminate a food choice that you think has a negative effect. Remove this food for two weeks and then introduce it slowly over a week. It is a similar process to when we are babies and foods are submitted to us slowly to see if we tolerate them well. Removing one thing at a time helps us determine some of the signals our body is telling us. It is essential to chart your process. Many of us think we will remember, but the clarity is often lost, and the Inspiration to continue is gone.

With holidays, parties, functions, etc., we will be surrounded by all the incredible delicacies and specially baked foods, deserts, and incredible foods. Many of them are family traditions, and we look forward to sharing them. This is part of indulgence that can be shared in a spiritual light—a great experience to connect and appreciate the senses on all levels.

Weight loss programs load up at the turn of a year with "New Year's Resolutions." Then they die in February, as the motivation quickly leaves many of us. What is left is the cycle of depression and disappointments once again. Another shift that offers a better chance at real success and lifestyle change is learning how to adjust the attitude around our energy. Goals are set to learn to eat the better choices that feed the real hunger. Witnessing our decisions and learning to listen to the more resounding voice is incredible. Having a better relationship with food can be much more exciting and fun, and our minds, bodies, and spirits can unite.

Be enlightened and encouraged by the quiet voice within, as it is our temple, our sanctuary of light, love, and natural healing. Please keep it simple, have fun, and enjoy the life of the physical, mental, and spiritual world. Find ways to help yourself achieve even the simplest of goals. Create new and healthy habits to get you on your way.

<u>Synthetic Hormones</u> in our internal and external environment are a huge concern, causing many of our health issues. That juicy steak or pig roast to those from the south, or the corn beef and hash or pot roast your momma made are loaded with them. Even the hamburgers and

the deli lunch meats add these imbalances to your body. Meat is loaded with synthetic chemicals.

It is no secret that the animals are given steroids to increase their rapid growth for profit. It is easy to bypass these thoughts and eat our favorites: prime rib, filet mignon, and brisket, to name a few. If we do this occasionally, there are other problems. Our body is better at cleansing them out in minimal amounts, so they don't build up and Cause damage. These chemicals are the internal beavers setting up where they choose, all over the body and brain.

Imagine this build-up of <u>synthetic chemicals</u> in any area they attach to. It is alarming if you allow yourself to stop and think about how it can relate to the current concerns like Heart Disease, Cancer, and Alzheimer's in our world today. There is evidence all around us and whether this is an everyday lifestyle. I encourage you to consider alternatives that can help your healing and return to some natural positive energy and quality of life. It is not impossible; we can alter things as we see our options. Everything in moderation was my father's favorite quote. It can shift once we let go, and we can feel invigorated and even have fun.

Clean, Clear, and Cleanse is the path to getting our body to remove them as fast as they come in from outside sources. It is a new way of thinking that has been missing for many years. Instant gratification has taken us to self-destruction. Suppose you are ready to roll up your sleeves and have fun seeing where you may never have been bold. Stay awake and keep looking and reading.

By learning to connect our minds to how food affects our health, we begin to understand what we need to avoid.

Here are some ideas to start with:

- Taking an inventory of the usual shopping list we do currently.
- Circle all the things that are your binge foods.
- Then the ones that you think are not healthy for you.

- Then highlight all the ones that you think are.
- Send a picture of this list to your accountability partner or Holistic Life Coach for suggestions to keep it exciting and fun.
- Add what you love that has become healthy for new ideas
- Create a list of what you may want to add as new things to try.

We look at the foods we love that we think are healthy and some we think are unhealthy. Then we look at the ones we want to buy even though they are not so great; we love them.

Looking at the breakdown of how to feed your body its basic needs will allow you to begin to help yourself make simple and new changes. Anywhere you start is a beginning, and think THINK THINK before it goes in the basket. Remind yourself that it is just for today, and for now, I want to see how good my body can feel from some of the efforts I put into these new choices.

Lose the words deserving and deprived for a while as well. Healing means a commitment, and for the 90 days of a new plan, this commitment can be taken one day at a time, One meal at a time, and one bite at a time.

TIP: *Try not to be hungry when you shop, as we tend to put* *those not- so-good choices in the basket and spend way more than we intended.*

Portion Control is Key, not only for the quantity of food but for training the eyesight to the plate. Eating enough to stimulate appetite, not sugar cravings

If you are still hungry, you eat the free foods on the list reference. Protein Options Daily women is around 46 grams

For Men, it is approximately 56 grams per day

A quick way to eye the right portion size is to make a fist that will be close to

3 -5 oz of meat

½ c of cooked grains and a slice of bread is one serving size

½ c pasta cooked is a serving size when trying to reduce simple carbs

Tips To save Money and Preplan Grass Fed Meats Look for sales and specials and buy to freeze for later.

MEN'S HEALTH Internal Restoration

Approaching healthier choices after years of neglect is the first step to healing the mind, body, and spirit. As the mood lifts and lightens, the body's wisdom tries to let us know if something we are doing doesn't sit right. It is common for many of us to live with various discomforts, often blamed on something other than the underlying cause. For example, if we have a diet high in simple carbohydrates, this causes inflammation in the body. This, in turn, breeds the onset of ailments, increases a person's pain levels, and can cause headaches and more severe migraines, hormonal imbalances, fatigue, and overall, less energy, higher acidic levels, acid reflux, and low oxygen levels. Etc. Removing these empty calories and choosing more nutrient-dense foods as part of the focus can help you get to the root causes and conditions.

Action is the key; it takes more than perfect conditions to take the first step. Think of a rainbow of colors in fruits and Veggies. Lean meats in a variety of choices throughout your week. This is important to keep your muscles and burn fat. Deep cold-water fish, kidney and navy beans, flax, and chia seeds (milled for best absorption) are good choices for a diet rich in essential Omega 3's. Magnesium is an important essential mineral (with a natural tranquilizing effect) found in dark green veggies, cereals, fish, nuts, and pumpkin seeds. Whole foods diets and an excellent real food multi-vitamin and mineral supplement are strongly advised for your Health Insurance Policy.

The top major health concerns today are heart disease, the onset of Diabetes 2, and Breast, Prostate, and Colon Cancer. Here are a few ideas on how to protect the internals. Tomatoes, due to Lycopene, help prevent cancer and tumor growth. Sulforaphane sources from Cruciferous Veggies help prevent cancer as well. Some are broccoli, cauliflower, brussels sprouts, rutabaga, cabbage, Bok choy, and kale). Green tea and pomegranates are great antioxidants to target and kill cancer cells and support healthy cells. If you like Indian food, turmeric is an excellent spice with many health benefits, and studies now show its prevention of tumor growth.

In later years, it is not uncommon for the prostate to sag due to the loss of muscle with aging. Best to stay fit now and work to keep your muscle mass to prevent more uncomfortable concerns later. Prostate health can also be protected by a supplement called Saw Palmetto, which is great for men over 50—not recommended for men planning on having children, as the semen potency levels can be affected negatively.

There are many ways to protect the health of the Colon. For best absorption, keep the digestive system healthy. Probiotics and Prebiotics (also known as the friendly guys) added to your digestive tract (Your Plumbing) will keep it healthy. These good bacteria help to ward off harmful bacteria, viruses, and other invaders, keeping the environment clean and protected.

It also helps to increase the Immune Health for the best absorption of your food. <u>Fiber</u> is essential for the daily elimination and cleansing of toxins. A diet rich in veggies, fruits, and whole grains will keep things moving. Some yogurts have good friendly bacteria but need more to keep a good balance in your plumbing. Ensure you drink sufficient purified water for proper hydration and flushing out toxins. Whatever your Current Body Weight is, cut that in half and drink that in ounces daily.

When preparing to have children, it is wise to plan two years to clean up your diet with good wholesome foods and take a multivitamin and mineral supplement to build healthy cells. Eating three meals daily and snacking between meals is a great way to keep your metabolism active and build good nutritional habits.

Heart Disease is an overall concern, especially moving into middle age. Cardio exercises are essential and needed to keep the heart muscle strong. A diet high in trans fats and overloaded with saturated fats over many years is an invitation to the onset of heart disease or a possible Heart Attack. Again, a diet rich in Omega 3s, calcium, magnesium, and good mono and polyunsaturated fats is vital to supporting your cardio health. Exercise is a challenge for many people. Some need extra support from a Personal Trainer to reach their goals. Suppose you add a workout for overall health. In that case, replacing fluids, you lose during exercise and protein (35 grams max) recovery shakes after activities are essential to maximizing the benefits.

Now the ever-important topic of testosterone and keeping the levels healthy. Keep in mind that your levels of Cortisol increase with stress and overload the adrenals. This makes it difficult to lose the extra pounds you carry and interferes with testosterone production (T- Levels). Healthy T- Levels have many essential roles in the body. In men, it helps regulate sex drive, bone strength, fat distribution, muscle mass, and strength. As men age, their life change, if you will, causes them to produce less testosterone. Some of it turns to estradiol, a form of estrogen; as men age, they make less of that. Eating foods rich in T- levels is the best way to protect your health.

Many men also experience Erectile Dysfunction, ED, and look for ways to increase the quality of their sex life with alternatives. Your blood work will help determine if it is due to low T levels. There ought to be careful consideration of prescription drugs as a choice. Some have lost their lives due to an unrecognizable heart condition. If you plan on going this route, please be up to date with a physical examination and have your doctor order a stress test to be sure your heart is in good condition. ED could indicate that something deeper is going on with your heart muscle. Since the blood vessels are so tiny that they carry blood to the penis, it is the first place to notice a possible underlying cause.

Are you over 40 and feeling run down and tired? Do you reach for the caffeine and sugary snacks for an afternoon pick-me-up? This may seem like a jolt, but it is often short-lived, and you may crash even harder. With the rise in Diabetes, this type of dietary intake, along with simple carbohydrates, overworks the pancreas and is a setup for the onset of Diabetes 2. Having fresh fruit for snacks and a cup of green or white tea instead can be healthy alternatives.

Stress: Critical Factors Highlighted

We can easily be caught in the stress trap and make the excuse to not take care of ourselves "because we are just too stressed." Sound familiar? We justify why we don't stop, but that keeps us from finding our path to protection during these times or cycles. Granted, it's a challenge for many of us, and the good news is, at the very least, we can be extra attentive to find simple things to do to help ride these times out. Even if it's years ahead, we must learn how to protect our health, hearts, and well-being. We stopped when we dropped in many cases, which was me.

One simple tool is to throw away the bat. Learning to not be hard on ourselves in our thoughts and knowing we are amongst the many who struggle with self-care and stress management.

A lot of us get off track until we fall from exhaustion. It may help to connect with where your body holds the stress. It can tell us that our body needs extra stress-managed care on that particular day or experience. Even if we can't stop burning the candle at both ends, we can learn self-care and stress management tools to meet our needs and protect our health. We can add many new and positive side effects daily to acknowledge the small steps and little victories!

Stress Management is the number one untreated problem

regarding our hormones. Of course, for our best health prevention, it is essential to reduce cortisol levels. Finding a way to give the body what it needs will offset its adverse effects on the imbalance of hormones or over-taxing the adrenals that can lead to Adrenal Fatigue.

Many issues also can be concerning with our adrenal glands.

When stress causes burnout through a lack of self-care, many concerns follow. For women during and transitioning through menopause, our adrenal glands work internally to assist in healing and protection. Many negative signs can be easily noticed when experiencing this concern, like hot flashes, losing hair, brittle nails, and dry skin. The doctor can test you if you request this.

A fact for women is the gradual or rapid or somewhere in between; the transition from the change in life from estrogen and protection falls away, and their role becomes the role of the adrenals. Managing stress responses and their length and severity in such conditions is increasingly important as we age.

Hormones for Healthy Balance Care

This is an important and complex subject. I will only touch on some of the following as a starting point for education. I will also add specific information for women and men that will follow.

Hormones for both men and women.

Testosterone has several functions. These hormones assist in muscle and bone growth. They also help with sex drive and help prevent aging later in life.

Dihydrotestosterone (DHT) has Several bodily functions, mainly the growth of muscles and bones. ...

Women's natural feminine health is balanced by estrogen and prostaglandins.

The Endocrine System is responsible for the release of hormones. The term to become aware of is endocrine disrupters. What are they, and how can we protect ourselves from them?

Iodine is a common element that Americans have become depleted in. Much of the American population has high blood pressure. Therefore, sodium and table salts are an increased risk for this category.

Consequently, many have become depleted in the Iodine

that is needed daily. One of the concerns is the thyroid gland, and its role is connected to many concerns if not given the Iodine to function as intended.

People with low levels of Iodine are linked to various problems. In my case, I had a swollen thyroid that I didn't notice myself. It was a centimeter more considerable than they liked, and the next step was a needle biopsy.

<u>Thyroid Goiters</u> are linked to Iodine deficiency. When getting a physical, the doctor checks the neck glands and thyroid to be sure nothing is swollen. I had done some of my research with the Naturopathic studies from doctors I follow and trust. I learned the problem is generally due to low levels of adequate Iodine, which is essential to the health of the

thyroid. I needed to take higher doses daily to return my body to the required level. It took about six months of attention to my body and thyroid to return to normal size. After mega dosing for about six months, I could taper off to a multi-vitamin pack. A patented formula designed to bypass the stomach acids directly to the small intestines that serve as a holding tank for all these nutrients released over the 24-hour timeframe on demand. My clients who have previously had stomach or digestive bypass surgeries have felt a significant change in as little as 30 days. Pretty incredible support for healing and the attempt to ensure our needs are met. I also enjoy the Himalayan pink salt for the various health benefits supporting HHR daily.

We need more stimulation if we are already highly agitated and running on adrenaline. The most obvious things to avoid are caffeinated coffee, tea, and energy drinks. Try swapping your usual brands for decaffeinated options or herbal teas like Chamomile.

<u>High carbs</u> foods are empty calories and become even more toxic to the body under stress. We are much more vulnerable to the breakdown of core physical energy and health as we lose the natural healthy "youth- like" power of rebounding sooner.

The bottom line is that there is nothing good or holistically healthy about hormone disruptors. So many other concerns, such as weight gain or loss, block our efforts to achieve the desired health. Stress management is crucial in supporting the overall health of our bodily functions.

Living with these concerns makes life so much harder to handle and can be avoided by simple substitutions for natural healing. You will learn about the alternatives by looking at your intake of hormones from the synthetic pool.

Decreasing the overall levels of synthetic hormones, the disruptors consumed daily, will improve your health and help your body to a healthier hormonal balance.

Summary

A great quote from recovery 12-step communities is remembering that we can move at our own pace. Here, the progressive state of movement finds acceptance in our now. Reducing our critical voices and negative thinking takes time. We can help ourselves shift from that mindset to move in this direction.

A message used in recovery to assist us in "Progress, not Perfection." This is not meant for the easy excuses to be lazy, but instead in the commitment to holistic health, moving at whatever pace keeps us going forward and out of stagnation.

1. Create simple, realistic goals to get started.
2. Be accountable to one another.
3. Any action is better than none. Baby steps.
4. Stick with people who strive for empowerment and the change you want.

With positive, healthy changes, we become walking testimonies to the people who love us, and your changes will speak at a higher volume than any words we can say.

Love for others can be a strong inspiration on the rougher days. However, self-motivation helps us build a more solid foundation.

Ultimately, from your positive self-care steps in action, no matter how small, the permission you give yourself is essential as you build the inner strength that no one can take or provide better than you.

An exercise reminder:

Take out your writing menus, journals, and folder from the beginning. Take your journal from the earlier work in the book that you may have started. If not before, start now to meet yourself here and now. If we still need to work together, I hope to meet with you to help you find your path to healing. It becomes inspiring to continue to look at what we have done as to what has worked and what doesn't. Our journey is ours; the rewards are new freedoms as we tune in and tap into what keeps us going.

This book provides information, resources, and guidance for holistic health practices. They are not intended to treat, diagnose, cure, or prevent any disease. Please get in touch with your medical team regarding suggestions or recommendations made in this book.

Conclusion

In all things new, we can come from our curious self to learn with fresh eyes from our spirit what is taking our self-care to another level and looking at all the parts of the soul, emotion, and physical and mental health. Learning to Nurture is the nature of all life, and much of life takes us away from this space to awaken these parts of who we are. So much of what we do is our norm. We can become very proud of the many accomplishments that we have achieved through our stepping stones. And there still may be a longing for something we are missing. Often it is the uncharted areas of our life we remove ourselves from for various reasons. The time may be now to explore what lights have been flickering and waiting for your nurturing time and self-care attention. The concept of healing is acknowledging it all and finding love and appreciation *for who we are and all we are, not just all we do*. Self- worth and compassion allow us to feel good and honored by our natural gifts. How many of them do we minimize because it comes easily to us?

Human nature does better when there is work and a commitment to building something to be proud of. But what gifts do you take for granted that you may not pay attention to or dismiss? Is there a passion we can learn about in them? As we awaken to live from our spirits as part of our purposeful life, we learn to appreciate taking self-care to another level.

Our inner strengths from our souls have much to teach us if we pay attention. We are also living in the <u>generation of our DNA family systems,</u> as science teaches us.

The body's memory could be another way to recognize some of the shadows in your way. Others can see, know and understand neglect or not caring, as in lack of motivation or understanding how much freedom will come in thriving for what we truly need to live our whole life.

Our complete healing of our mind-body-spirit can be at the lasting life changes that often happen automatically as we open to simple and new ideas. From our inner lifestyles, we can still spread collective unity with ourselves and others to reach heights we never knew we could. How much can we offer one another as we hear these new ideas through exciting opportunities that can awaken the spirit or better self to get our attention? Slowly but steadily, as at a turtle's pace, with an

understanding that healing is a natural gift and tapping into this awareness can be the change to eternal life right here on earth. Getting support in the more profound healing modalities can offer tools and new skills to ride these times out, as I referred to in my story a the beginning. We are getting some of our shadows out into the light for healing. Surprisingly, we no longer need to carry them and can find forgiveness.

Acknowledgments

I have continued Inspiration and deep appreciation for my family: Father ~ Fred J Russell, 11; Mother ~ Patricia Courshon Russell; Siblings/Nieces & Nephews~ Fredrick J Russell, 111, and his wife, our bonus sister Gail, Rick (Elaina) Daniel, Joanna Russell Kopsaftis, (Jim) Gayle H. Russell, James Russell, Patricia Russell Dallinga and her husband, our brother Tom, Jessica, and Jenna. Dallinga. The next generation of cousins: Camilla, Addison, Alexandra, Angelina, Shane, and the twins Nolan, Lia, and all the souls to follow.

My cup runneth over for my incredible son Paul James Crossan, his wife Kristi Lynne, and my loving granddaughter Angelina Jamie Crossan. Your love story is fantastic, and I thank God for your perseverance in the life you are building with your family. You all have filled my heart with richness; I love you all and am grateful beyond.

Immense love for Heather Bunnenburg Duffelmeyer and her husband (Richie), My daughter from another mother, babysitter to Paul James beginning in Yonkers, NY, at three years old, sister, and loyal, loving best friend. Many seasons we have been through, and her love and light met my soul from day one over 40 years ago. My heart is fuller and more prosperous because of all you are, with Grace, to keep thriving. Nana to their children, Richie, Ryan, and Rylee. Love also to her twin sister Lauralee and her daughter Katelyn. God's Grace continues to shine for them all.

Special Acknowledgement to my Warrior sisters of over 35 years, still thriving and healing friendships; Jody I, Shelly S, Kimberly S, Sharon M, and Cori E; without their unconditional love, guidance, and support, I would not be here today!

Terry Minervini, my longest and best friend from three years old. A lifetime of joy in my heart, and to date, the memories are priceless. I loved my Youth when I could get away and spend time with her family home away from home and her grandfather's cabin at Candlewood Knolls in New Fairfield, Connecticut. We had loads of fun, with lots of laughter and love. I am proud to call her my longest lifelong friend.

To another lifelong friend Cathy Dolan O'Brien, and her husband Ed, through all the many seasons of our lives to date. Cathy has always been unconditionally loving, kind, and patient with me, and heart of gold. And I am proud to have had her friendship for over 50 years! Much of this book was written in their NY home, as they gifted me a new laptop, so I could keep writing. So blessed to be part of their growing family from her son William (Rebecca) 2, Rachael 2, Jessica 3, and my God Son Eddie (Jackie) 4, a total of 11 grandchildren: love to them all.

I appreciate and love Duane Deorka for his light always being on for me. In my early teens, I wandered and waited for him; his door was always open. Our friendship from then until now is heartwarming, and I look forward to more memories as we travel. Love, Love, Love!

Stephanie Kilcoyne Alter, our memories are fantastic. My first and only adult trip to Capistrano Beach, California, is among the fondest. We had some crazy fun on our adventures. We met in Rockaway Beach to give us something to do and avoid trouble. Instead, we found it right from the start. Love you and hold you close at heart.

Joey A, my best friend for over 50 years. So very glad we stayed in touch and remained friends. A voice of reason and truth always, A brother from another mother, with love and a grateful heart! The past ten years of reconnecting have been a gift to my spirit. I appreciate the support and love!

Thankful to my beautiful friend from High School, Patty Vergottini Brown, for constantly pushing me to find the strength she saw in me. A huge turn of events happened that last time I stood at the crossroads of uncertainty. With Patty's encouragement, I applied for a manager's job in the South Salam, NY, food business and was hired. I met Robert T at the most crucial point in my life.

I am reconnecting with Eddie R and am thankful to share healing time and laughter in recent calls. I greatly appreciate life cycles that offer joy to my spirit and remind me of our great memories. I always wish him love and light in his musical adventures with incredible talents.

Robert T, (RIP) Lynn, Bobby K, Shirley E, Duane D, Eddie R, Elizabeth W, Anne O, Patty K, Jenny S, (RIP) Gerri S, (RIP) Patricia L, Nancy J, Sharon M, Donna S, Betsy M, Dori S, Cynthia G, Janet B, Jody I, Nancy Lee S, (RIP) Stacey N, Kristi N, Roseanne L; Vincent H, my almost-husband, I love you all …. to the moon and beyond. For those not mentioned, you know who you are, Bedford Community Church 1987. The paradigm shifts, and spiritual connection gave me a real life. May Grace, love, and light be with you all. Passing it on :-)

Not enough words to express the patience, tolerance, love, guidance, and support from my mentor Suzie Sunkel for over 30 years and still counting. Thank you so much for all your unconditional love and special friendship—a recent donation to own the book rights for my labor of love and Grace. I can always count on the truth between my eyes when I need it most. I have been so blessed to have her guidance and unconditional love.

JeAnne M from Life Recovery weekly Sundays at 7:00 pm est. She has been my earthly angel in the last transition of my life to date, and so grateful for her love, guidance, prayers, and friendship. Tracy C, Penelope KC, Mary Ellen S, Diane T, and the collective energy we share as we all grow on the Global Virtual Support Meetings for all walks of life offered daily. Thank you all for the gifts of Grace to date, and you all continue to give much love, healing, and light collectively.

An incredible spirit of love and Grace and so much support for me. Through the last three years and still growing strong, Chrissy F has given unconditionally and financially as a donation from her heart, pocketbook, and giving nature. She has made my life healing on the farm better through some of the darker times, and I am forever grateful.

Another appreciation to the founders of the intherooms.com, Ron T and Kenny P, whom I was fortunate to meet at the <u>Unite Recovery Rally in Washington, DC, in 2014.</u>

Several serve to support recovery lifestyles on various platforms. <u>Sofia Caudle-</u>Grief and Co-Dependency is a weekly group meeting on Wednesdays at noon. Trauma and Recovery meetings on Wednesdays at 8:30 pm est. They are for open sharing, or anonymous, with the dedicated host Barb. Also, Rachel Leavy with Healthy Love meets weekly on Thursdays at 9:00 pm est. You can find all resources at the site www.intherooms.com. Look for the full schedule from the site's home page.

Special appreciation to the contributors; this book would not have been published without their kindness and support: Dr.

Wayne Franklin and his lovely wife, Marian O'Connor Franklin, Christina Figueroa, and Suzie Sunkel. I love and appreciate you all beyond words.

Michelle C. Spuck, Author of <u>Heal the Body Honor the Soul</u>, for an incredible earth angel in my life for over 36 years. We have been truly blessed and inspired as we continue sharing our journey.

My Coach and Assessment Editor, Martha E. Lang. This was only possible with her guidance and lengthy re-structuring abilities. She softly pushed and inspired me to where I didn't know I could go. Much love and appreciation for your guidance and support through this new beginning as an Author to follow Grace and the calling to help others.

Blessings to all for Healing Light within, Kathy

About Author

The Author, Kathleen, shares her foundations of growing up in a dysfunctional home life and how this wreaked havoc on her brain, body, and spirit. Her struggles were many, and she did not understand how much they hindered her life. Like most in her situation, her lack of attention and focus were insurmountable through the trauma responses left, in her body and mind, which later dictated her life's direction. You will read about when she reached the age of 30, everything in her life became clear and her second chances were unfolding continually for over 36 years.

Her passion has been the integration of how body, mind and spirit callings have been missed with old thinking habits and self-destruction and messages that were hidden in the clouds. She shares her wealth of knowledge from her firsthand experience that led her to higher callings, wisdom, and insight for herself and helping others. This book encapsulates information and educational guidance on our relationship to self-love and self-care affects all our systems, how each one heals, and how using these guides can help us to reach endless possibilities for healing.

Resources and References

Author Gordon Ross Hutchison (Offered Recipes Appendix 11)

https://www.kirkusreviews.com/book-reviews/gordon-hutchison/gangsters-geishas-monks-me/

Support Recovery for you and your family

www.intherooms.com Articles, Recovery Connections, Live Anonymous meetings, Treatment Centers, Global Support, and More!

Domestic Violence

https://www.thehotline.org/

Alcoholics Anonymous

www.aa.org

Narcotics Anonymous

www.na.org

Al-Anon/Al-Ateen

www.alanon.org

Nar Anon

www.nar-anon.org

Gamblers Anonymous

https://www.gamblersanonymous.org/ga/

Sex and Love Addiction

https://slaafws.org/

Adult Children of Alcoholics and Dysfunctional Homes (ACA)

www.adultchildren.org

Overeaters Anonymous

http://oa.org

New Life Recovery

www.liferecoverygroups.com

Sex and Love Addiction Treatment Facility Dr. Rob Weiss MSW

https://seekingintegrity.com/

Codependency CODA

coda.org

Grief and Codependency Relationships Dr. Sophia

Shop Page on her website

Healthy Love Rachael Leavy Psychotherapy

Website for more information

Contact Information for the Author

https://openroadsmrkt.wixsite.com/nutritional-healing

www.ingramcontent.com/pod-product-compliance
Lightning Source LLC
Chambersburg PA
CBHW042335150426
43194CB00005B/163